Dream BIG American Idol SUPERSTARS

Kris Allen

David Archuleta

Kelly Clarkson

David Cook

Chris Daughtry

Jennifer Hudson

Adam Lambert

Kellie Pickler

Jordin Sparks

Carrie Underwood

Elliott Yamin

American Idol Profiles Index:
Top Finalists from Seasons 1 to 7
(82 Contestants)

Insights Into American Idol

Carrie Underwood

Hal Marcovitz

Mason Crest Publishers

Produced by 21st Century Publishing and Communications, Inc.

MASON CREST PUBLISHERS INC.
370 Reed Road
Broomall, Pennsylvania 19008
(866) MCP-BOOK (toll free)
www.masoncrest.com

Printed in the United States of America.

First Printing

9 8 7 6 5 4 3 2 1

Library of Congress Cataloging-in-Publication Data

Marcovitz, Hal.
    Carrie Underwood / Hal Marcovitz.
        p. cm.—(Dream big: American Idol superstars)
    Includes bibliographical references and index.
    ISBN 978-1-4222-1512-8 (hardback : alk. paper)
    ISBN 978-1-4222-1594-4 (pbk. : alk. paper)
    1. Underwood, Carrie, 1983–   —Juvenile literature. 2. Singers—United States—
Biography—Juvenile literature. I. Title.
ML3930.U53M37 2010   .
782.421642092—dc22
    [B]   2009021191

CONTENTS

American Idol TIMELINE

October 5, 2001

Pop Idol, a TV reality show created by Simon Fuller, debuts in the United Kingdom and becomes a smash hit.

Fall 2001

Based on the success of *Pop Idol*, and after initially rejecting the concept, FOX Network agrees to buy *American Idol*, a national talent competition and TV reality show.

Spring 2002

Auditions for *American Idol* Season 1 are held in New York City, Los Angeles, Chicago, Dallas, Miami, Atlanta, and Seattle.

January 21, 2003

American Idol Season 2 premieres without Brian Dunkleman, leaving Ryan Seacrest as the sole host.

May 21, 2003

- *American Idol* Season 2 finale airs.
- Ruben Studdard narrowly wins and Clay Aiken is the runner-up.
- Runner-up Clay Aiken goes on to become extremely successful both critically and commercially.

January 19, 2004

American Idol Season 3 premieres.

2001   2002   2003   2004

June 11, 2002

American Idol Season 1 premieres on FOX Network, with Simon Cowell, Paula Abdul, and Randy Jackson as the judges, and Ryan Seacrest and Brian Dunkleman as the co-hosts.

September 4, 2002

- *American Idol* Season 1 finale airs.
- Kelly Clarkson wins and Justin Guarini is the runner-up.
- Kelly Clarkson goes on to become the most successful Idol winner and a superstar in the music industry.

Fall 2002

Auditions for *American Idol* Season 2 are held in New York City, Los Angeles, Miami, Detroit, Nashville, and Austin.

January 27, 2004

William Hung's audition is aired and his humble response to Simon Cowell's scathing criticism make William the most famous American Idol non-qualifier and earn him record deals and a cult-like following.

April 21, 2004

Jennifer Hudson is voted off the show in 7th place, and goes on to win the role of Effie in *Dreamgirls*, for which she wins an Academy Award, a Golden Globe Award, and a Grammy Award.

May 26, 2004

- *American Idol* Season 3 finale airs with 65 million viewers casting their votes.
- Fantasia Barrino is crowned the winner and Diana DeGarmo is the runner-up.
- Fantasia soon becomes the first artist in the history of Billboard to debut at number one with her first single.

May 10, 2006

Chris Daughtry is voted off the show in 4th place, and soon after forms the band, Daughtry, and releases its debut album, which becomes number one on the charts, wins many awards, and finds huge commercial success.

April 26, 2006

Kellie Pickler is voted off the show in 6th place, and soon releases her debut album, which rockets to number one on the Billboard Top Country Album chart.

January 17, 2006

American Idol Season 5 premieres and for the first time airs in high definition.

May 24, 2006

- *American Idol* Season 5 finale airs.
- Taylor Hicks is the winner and Katharine McPhee the runner-up.
- Elliot Yamin, the second runner-up, goes on to release his debut album, which goes gold.

January 16, 2007

American Idol Season 6 premieres.

April 2007

The *American Idol* Songwriting Contest is announced.

January 15, 2008

American Idol Season 7 airs with a four-hour two-day premiere.

April 9, 2008

Idol Gives Back returns for its second year.

May 21, 2008

- *American Idol* Season 7 finale airs.
- David Cook wins with 54.6 million votes and David Archuleta is the runner-up with 42.9 million votes.
- Both Davids go on to tremendous post-Idol success with successful albums and singles.

2005   2006   2007   2008   2009

May 25, 2005

- *American Idol* Season 4 finale airs.
- Carrie Underwood wins and Bo Bice is the runner-up.
- Carrie goes on to become one of the most successful Idol winners, selling millions of albums and winning scores of major awards.

January 18, 2005

- *American Idol* Season 4 premieres.
- Some rules change:
  - The age limit is raised from 24 to 28.
  - The semi-final competition is separated by gender up until the 12 finalists.

April 24–25, 2007

American Idol Gives Back, a charitable campaign to raise money for underprivileged children worldwide, airs, and raises more than $70 million.

May 23, 2007

- *American Idol* Season 6 finale airs.
- Jordin Sparks wins with 74 million votes and Blake Lewis is the runner-up.
- Jordin goes on to join Kelly Clarkson and Carrie Underwood in the ranks of highly successful post-Idol recording artists.

January 13, 2009

American Idol Season 8 premieres adding Kara DioGuardi as a fourth judge.

February 14, 2009

The American Idol Experience, a theme park attraction, officially opens at Disney's Hollywood Studio in Florida.

May 20, 2009

- *American Idol* Season 8 finale airs.
- Kris Allen unexpectedly wins and Adam Lambert is the runner-up.
- Almost 100 million people voted in the season 8 finale.

Carrie Underwood can no longer contain herself after winning five Billboard Music Awards in 2006. After having won *American Idol* Season 4, Carrie was swept away on a whirlwind journey that would eventually lead her to becoming one of the brightest superstars of the music world.

1

Carrie's Whirlwind Journey

Even though *American Idol* judge Simon Cowell forecast big things for Carrie Underwood, nearly everybody in the music industry was truly shocked by the success of Carrie's first album, *Some Hearts*. The album sold 300,000 copies in its first week and would eventually go 7-times **platinum**, selling more than 7 million copies, and winning numerous prestigious awards.

The album also proved to be a crossover hit. Soon after its release, *Some Hearts* earned a No. 2 ranking on the pop music charts as well as a No. 1 ranking on the country charts, making it the top-selling debut album in the history of country music.

9

Clearly, the album owed much of its success to Carrie's popularity as the reigning winner on *American Idol*. Just months before the album's November 2005 release, Carrie had been voted winner of the nationwide talent competition, thanks mostly to a dedicated legion of fans struck by the singer's sizzling talent and traffic-stopping beauty.

And that is why, as the *American Idol* competition moved into its final weeks, Simon found himself making this prediction:

> **❝Carrie, you're not just the girl to beat, you're the person to beat. I will make a prediction, not only will you win this competition, but you will sell more records than any other previous *Idol* winner.❞**

THE FIRST *AMERICAN IDOL* WINNER KELLY CLARKSON

Simon Cowell's prediction that Carrie Underwood's albums would outsell the music produced by all other *American Idol* winners has not quite come true. Although Carrie's album *Some Hearts* did sell more than 7 million copies, its sales rank far behind *Breakaway*, the second album recorded by 2002 *American Idol* winner Kelly Clarkson. Kelly's *Breakaway* has sold more than 13 million copies.

Kelly was the first winner of the national competition. After growing up in the small town of Joshua, Texas, Kelly turned down college scholarships and instead moved to Los Angeles, California, where she hoped to break into the music industry. After Kelly performed in one of the early elimination rounds of *American Idol*, all judge Randy Jackson could find to say was, "Kelly, Kelly, Kelly. Very, very, very, very, good."

Long Weekend in Nashville

The songs for *Some Hearts* were selected over a long weekend that summer in Nashville, Tennessee, the capital of country music. Simon Fuller, the creator of *American Idol* and head of

19 Management, the producer of the album, drafted some of the best country music songwriters in the business. He arranged for them to meet with Carrie so she could hear their songs and pick the music that best suited her singing style.

Carrie is a full-voiced singer who brings a lot of emotion to her performances. Among the tracks selected for the album were "Jesus Take the Wheel," in which a young mother finds her life slipping out of control; "Before He Cheats," a defiant ballad about

Carrie performs onstage at the 2006 CMT Music Awards. Her full-range voice and emotion-packed singing style, which led her to being crowned the *American Idol* winner, are also showcased in her debut album, *Some Hearts*. The album rocketed to the top of the charts and would eventually sell millions of copies.

a woman seeking revenge against a cheating boyfriend; and the title track, "Some Hearts," a love song with a bouncy beat. Carrie also contributed music and lyrics for one of the tracks on the album, "I Ain't in Checotah Anymore," a song about her hometown in Oklahoma and the whirlwind journey she has taken since winning *American Idol*. Said Carrie,

> **"Writing songs is always something that I have been interested in, but I really didn't feel like my writing chops were good enough yet to write songs for my first album. I did, however, try my best to help. I wanted to help write a song that was strictly for my friends and family in my hometown of Checotah. . . . It's basically an account of the things that have been happening to me over the past few months."**

Critical Success

Some Hearts turned out to be both a commercial and a critical success. In the year or so after the album's release, Carrie won awards from the Academy of Country Music as Top New Female Vocalist and Top Female Vocalist, while "Jesus Take the Wheel" was cited by the academy as Single Record of the Year and *Some Hearts* won Album of the Year. Also, Carrie won a Grammy Award for Best Female Country Performance while "Jesus Take the Wheel" won for Best Country Song.

But perhaps her biggest night occurred on December 4, 2006, when Carrie and *Some Hearts* won five trophies at the Billboard Music Awards, including Album of the Year, Country Album of the Year, Female Billboard 200 Artist of the Year, Female Country Artist of the Year, and New Country Artist of the Year. On that night, a national television audience watched as Carrie made several trips to the stage at the MGM Grand Garden Arena in Las Vegas, Nevada, to accept her honors. She said,

An emotional Carrie thanks her supporters as she accepts the Album of the Year award for *Some Hearts* at the 2006 Academy of Country Music Awards. The album, applauded by critics and fans alike, also became a huge commercial success for the young singer.

"This is not only incredible for me, but this is incredible for country music. I want to thank God, I want to thank the fans, of course; I want to thank each and every artist that's out there tonight putting out great music. You guys are awesome, and you're making the world a better place. So thank everybody at my label, Arista, everybody at 19 Management, of course *American Idol*—just all you guys rock. Thank you."

Carrie grew up in Checotah, Oklahoma, where she helped her father on the family ranch. Although she always sang in the choir and school musicals, no one in her small town would have guessed she would someday be a glamorous singing sensation!

2

Girl from Checotah

Carrie first sang in public at the age of three, giving a performance at church. Her talent was obvious, and she continued singing in church and school choirs, often winning the lead roles in school musicals. Throughout this time, the only voice lessons Carrie received were from her middle school choir director, who taught her how to breathe between notes.

Despite her strong voice and musical gift, Carrie's talent often went unnoticed in her hometown of Checotah. As a young girl, she entered many talent competitions but never won first prize. Often, she went home with second or third prize—usually a $25 U.S. Savings Bond. Recalled Carrie,

15

> **"I competed in a lot of stuff, and I didn't win. Ever. I never won a single one. That was when I was 12, 13, 14 years old. But I didn't need to win. If I got third and got a little trophy or money for school, that made me happy."**

Musically Talented

Carrie was born March 10, 1983, in Muskogee, a small town in Oklahoma. She is the youngest of three daughters born to Stephen and Carole Underwood. When Carrie was still a young girl, her father retired from his job at a paper mill and bought a ranch in nearby Checotah. Carrie grew up on the ranch, helping her father tend the cattle in the mornings, then hurrying off to school where she was an honor student. "I was definitely a tomboy," Carrie said. "I climbed trees, and I'd jump hay bales and play with the cows, and Dad would take me fishing."

As a young girl, Carrie listened to the music her parents enjoyed—songs by the Beatles, Creedence Clearwater Revival,

CARRIE UNDERWOOD: AN OKIE FROM MUSKOGEE

Carrie was born in a town made famous in a 1969 song by country star Merle Haggard, "Okie from Muskogee." It is a humorous song that salutes rural life and small-town values. The song has become a classic of country music, recorded by many artists over the years.

The song was originally recorded during an era when young people questioned authority and protested the Vietnam War. "Okie from Muskogee" was regarded as an answer to the anti-war movement and the rebelliousness of the times. The song includes the lyrics "we don't let our hair grow long and shaggy, like the hippies out in San Francisco do." Haggard has always maintained that he wrote the song as a joke and never expected it to gain widespread popularity.

The Oklahoma Music Hall of Fame is located in a former train depot in Muskogee. Although Haggard was born in California, in 1997 he was selected as one of the initial inductees into the Hall of Fame for helping popularize the state by recording "Okie from Muskogee."

Carrie first sang in church at age three and later came to love gospel music. At an early age, it was clear that Carrie had a musical gift. She often entered local talent competitions and always had a great time, even if she didn't win first place.

and the Bee Gees, among others. Her older sisters, Shanna and Stephanie, were fans of the **heavy metal** bands of the 1980s, and they chuckled as their baby sister would sing along with the screaming, head-banging singers of such groups as Mötley Crüe and Metallica.

Soon, Carrie developed her own tastes in music. Brought up in a strict Baptist home, Carrie developed a love for **gospel music** but was soon drawn to country as well. As a teenager, she grew very fond of the songs of country stars Reba McEntire, Faith Hill, and Martina McBride.

INFLUENCED BY MARTINA McBRIDE

During the 1990s, Martina McBride was among a new wave of country recording stars who found so-called crossover appeal—their music was embraced by country fans as well as pop music fans. When Carrie was asked by judge Randy Jackson during her *Idol* audition to name her favorite singer, Carrie immediately answered Martina McBride.

Born Martina Mariea Schiff in 1966 in the small town of Medicine Lodge, Kansas, Martina broke into recording in 1992 when she released the album *The Time Has Come*, which included the single "Independence Day." The controversial song, which Carrie performed in final round of *American Idol*, tells the story about an abused wife seeking revenge against her husband by burning their home to the ground. Since the release of *The Time Has Come*, Martina has blossomed into one of the music industry's biggest stars, selling more than 16 million albums.

At the age of 14, a family friend arranged for Carrie to audition for executives at Capitol Records, one of the top record companies in the country. To audition, she traveled to Nashville but the tryout never panned out. Looking back on the experience, Carrie knows that at the age of 14, she wouldn't have been ready for the fast-paced lifestyle of a recording star. She said,

❝**I honestly think it's a lot better that nothing came out of it now, because I wouldn't have been ready then. Everything has a way of working out.**❞

Pizza Shop Waitress

Otherwise, music played a small role in her life. At Checotah High School, she played softball and basketball, joined the cheerleading squad, and paid attention to her studies. She also developed a love for animals, and at the age of 13 became a **vegetarian**. Mostly, Carrie remembers her years at Checotah High as fun but hardly exciting. She recalled,

> **"In high school there wasn't that much to do. If we were going to go out, we'd just go see a movie. My junior or senior year we got a bowling alley put in, so sometimes we'd go bowling. I wasn't too bad, if I do say so myself. Usually, I bowled a 130."**

Like Carrie, music superstar Maria McBride came from a small town in the Midwest and took the music industry by storm. During Carrie's *American Idol* audition, she called Maria her favorite singer, and she was proud to perform Maria's song, "Independence Day," in her final *Idol* round.

After high school in Checotah, Carrie gave up her dream of singing while working and attending college. She held several jobs that helped pay tuition but didn't inspire her. If she hadn't auditioned for *American Idol,* she might have left music behind for good and never fulfilled her dream.

In 2001, she graduated as her high school **salutatorian**, then entered college at Northeastern State University in Tahlequah, Oklahoma, about an hour's drive from Checotah. In college, she majored in broadcast journalism. Carrie saw herself as a TV reporter or in a behind-the-scenes technical job. She helped produce TV shows for the campus television station and contributed stories for the school newspaper. She was a good student who scored high grades, joined a sorority to get over her shyness, and started doing charity work. Some of her public service activities included volunteering to collect litter along the highways and visiting **hospice** patients. "In a roomful of people, she wouldn't be one you would hear a lot of," recalled Suzanne Myers, one of Carrie's professors at Northeastern State. "She's not the life of the party. She's just very sweet."

Meanwhile, Carrie also held a number of part-time jobs to help pay for her **tuition** at Northeastern State. She worked as a waitress at a local pizza shop and also held jobs at a zoo and veterinary clinic. One summer, she worked as a **page** for an Oklahoma state legislator. Except for doing some singing and dancing for an amateur theater in Tahlequah, music was far from her mind. She said,

> **"After high school, I pretty much gave up on the dream of singing. I had reached a point in my life where I had to be practical and prepare for my future in the 'real world.'"**

In the summer of 2002, just after finishing her freshman year at Northeastern State, Carrie found a job as a cashier at Albert's One Stop, a local gas station. That summer, as Carrie worked behind the cash register at Albert's, a new TV show debuted on the Fox network. It was called *American Idol*.

Carrie's road to stardom began in 2004 with her first *Idol* audition in St. Louis, Missouri, with thousands of other hopeful performers. When the judges told her she would be going on to Hollywood, she joyfully rushed out of the room to hug her mother, who had driven her all the way from Oklahoma.

3

The Road to Stardom

In the fall of 2004, as Carrie was preparing to enter her final semester in college, she learned that auditions would be held for the fourth season of *American Idol*. She thought over the notion of auditioning for the competition and decided to go for it. Carrie's mother volunteered to drive her the 400 miles to St. Louis, Missouri, to participate in the first round of tryouts.

American Idol

American Idol premiered in 2002 on American TV—it was based on a similar show, *Pop Idol*, that made its debut a year before on British TV. The show became an immediate hit among American audiences. Each year, the audience expanded;

during the season that Carrie competed more than 500 million people tuned in.

Preliminary auditions are held in several cities across the country. In addition to St. Louis, in the year in which Carrie competed auditions were also held in Cleveland, Ohio; Las Vegas, Nevada; New Orleans, Louisiana; Orlando, Florida; San Francisco, California; and Washington, D.C. Once word gets out that *Idol* producers are auditioning talent, it is not unusual for thousands of would-be entertainers to line up for hours, waiting for their one brief shot at stardom. That certainly happened during the 2005 competition—some 100,000 people tried out in all seven cities. Like all the others who auditioned, Carrie had to wait in line as well.

The first round of auditions are always held in front of producers who give each contestant just seconds to sing a few bars of music. If they survive two rounds in front of the producers, the contestants are invited back a third time to perform for judges Simon Cowell, Randy Jackson, and Paula Abdul. If the contestants impress the judges, they are invited to Hollywood to take part in the actual, week-by-week competitions.

WHO ARE THE JUDGES?

When Carrie first met judges Simon Cowell, Paula Abdul, and Randy Jackson, she admitted to being nervous because she found Simon "scary." Indeed, Simon has earned himself a reputation as a wisecracking and sarcastic judge who can be truly vicious toward contestants.

Born in Great Britain, Simon is a veteran music industry insider who started judging talent on *Pop Idol*, the British version of *American Idol*, in 2001. As for the other judges, Randy is a Grammy Award-winning music producer, as well as a musician, singer, and radio host, while Paula is a former Los Angeles Lakers cheerleader who went on to become a singer, dancer, and choreographer. Her 1988 album, *Forever Your Girl*, made it to the top of the *Billboard* charts. For the 2009 season, the *American Idol* executives added a fourth judge to the panel, singer and songwriter Kara DioGuardi.

If *American Idol* contestants make it through two auditions for the show's producers, they perform for three judges (from left): Randy Jackson, Paula Abdul, and Simon Cowell. These three decide who will go on to Hollywood, and they also criticize or praise the contestants on the televised *Idol* episodes.

First Round Audition

At her initial audition in front of one of the show's producers, Carrie sang Martina McBride's "Phones Are Ringing All Over Town." Although she didn't think the audition went very well, she was invited back the next day for the second round. This time, she sang another Martina McBride song, "Independence Day." Again, she was invited back, this time to audition for Simon, Randy, and Paula. Said Carrie,

After a long car ride and even longer wait in line, a tired and discouraged Carrie didn't think her first *American Idol* audition went well. To her surprise, she was asked back for a second and third round. Win or lose, she had decided to always give it her best shot.

❝Once my mother agreed to drive me, we had to wait there forever. . . . We hopped in a car and drove all night. I was then one of the last people to audition in St. Louis, so I had to wait for many hours. I was so tired when I finally got to audition. I'm not sure what they saw in me, but I am grateful for this opportunity.❞

As the time neared for her audition before the judges, Carrie paced nervously up and down the hallway of the St. Louis hotel where the tryouts were staged. Finally, she was called in to perform. She admitted to being nervous, but then belted out several bars of "I Can't Make You Love Me" by folk-rocker Bonnie Raitt. Clearly, the judges were impressed. Simon said, "I'm surprised we haven't found a good country singer in this competition." After a quick vote by the judges, Randy said, "Welcome to Hollywood, girl." Carrie dashed out of the ballroom and hugged her mother.

Her decision to compete on *Idol* meant dropping out of college just short of her degree, but Carrie decided that she would have one shot at stardom and now was the time to take it. She said,

❝I thought, 'I'm about to graduate and I don't know what I'm going to do, so why not try out for *American Idol*? What's the worst that could happen? If I don't make it past the audition, nobody's going to know. And I'll get some experience in front of the camera.❞

Small-Town Girl in Hollywood

Soon after Carrie arrived in Hollywood to compete on *American Idol*, the show's host, Ryan Seacrest, asked her if she had seen any stars. No, Carrie answered, it had been too cloudy. Ryan laughed and pointed out that he didn't mean the stars in the sky, he meant movie stars.

Clearly, Carrie was a small-town girl who found the sights and sounds of the big city overwhelming. After all, she had never been far from home. In fact, when she boarded the flight to Los Angeles, it was the first time in her life that she had taken an airplane ride.

Even after arriving in Hollywood, Carrie found it difficult to shake off her small-town ways. The *Idol* producers gave the contestants money to spend on clothes. While some of the other contestants trotted off to the chic boutiques in Beverly Hills, Carrie spent her money frugally, shopping at some of the less-expensive stores. Her plan was to save the money and, after she was voted off the show, use it to help pay her college tuition. She said,

> **We were given a budget to shop, but it wasn't much, especially for Los Angeles. I was saving every penny I could from any money I got from the show. I thought, 'I'll put this away, and I can go finish college after it's over,' because I never expected to win. My thoughts were, 'There's no way I'm going to drop $800 on a dress.' That's silly.**

Broadway Tunes and Oldies

Each season of *American Idol* actually starts out on a humorous note, as viewers get to see some of the less-talented performers sing for the judges, but once the show moves on to Hollywood the series evolves into a serious competition among the talented finalists.

The show airs two nights a week. Although the rules are tweaked from year to year, the contestants always perform on the first night for the judges. If the judges approve, the singers move on to the second night where they perform again, and this time, the national TV audience members vote over the phone for their favorite performers. Over the years, different variations of "wildcard" rounds and other second-chance competitions have

Carrie got into the *Idol* competition by singing country music favorites, but in later rounds she stretched herself to include Broadway tunes, disco, rock, dance music, and oldies. Carrie worried about her abilities in some of these areas, but loyal fans continued to support her and voted her into the finals.

given performers opportunities to return to the contests even though they may have failed to impress the judges or received low vote totals from TV viewers.

In the year in which Carrie competed, by the time the show moved into its semifinal round she found herself competing against 23 other contestants—11 other women and 12 men. Each week, the bottom two competitors were eliminated until just 12 performers remained for the finals.

Once in the finals, the competitors are required to sing music outside their strongest genres. Certainly, Carrie made it into the competition by singing a heavy dose of country music, but after the finals got underway she was required to sing Broadway tunes, oldies, and dance music. She found herself belting out hits by 1960s **rockabilly** star Roy Orbison, 1970s **disco** queen Donna Summer, 1980s rocker Pat Benatar, and the 1990s soft rock group Air Supply. Said Carrie,

> **"Millions of people all over the U.S. saw me do my best and my worst week to week on the show."**

Carrie had to get used to signing autographs. During the competitions, some loyal fans threw stuffed teddy bears onto the stage and were soon called the "Care Bears." Most admirers were polite, but sometimes Carrie was uncomfortable with "creepy" fans who intruded into her personal life.

Brink of Stardom

As the competition headed into the finals, which occur over the last 11 weeks of the season, Carrie clearly emerged as a front-runner. Fans seemed to support Simon's prediction that she would not only win but also become a top-selling recording star. In fact, during the finals, Carrie never finished in the bottom three of the voting—a distinction held only by Kelly Clarkson, the first season's winner, and Clay Aiken, the runner-up in season two.

THE "CARE BEARS"

As she started moving through the *American Idol* competition and establishing herself as one of the top contenders, Carrie found herself with a legion of loyal fans. During her performances, fans often tossed stuffed teddy bears onto stage, earning themselves the nickname of the "Care Bears."

Carrie said she is constantly shocked that fans would want her autograph—particularly fans back home in Checotah. "People I've known my whole life asked for my autograph," she said. "I'm like, 'That's silly.' Why do you want my name on a piece of paper?"

On the other hand, Carrie has also had some experiences with creepy fans. She recalled,

" Ninety-nine percent of my fans are great, loyal, normal, wonderful fans. Then there's that one fan that crosses the line. . . . My grandmother recently passed away, and there was a person who came to the cemetery to take pictures . . . I hid at first, and then my brother-in-law said, 'Do you want me to go talk to him?' So he went over to the guy, and the guy was like, 'Oh, I'm sorry. . . .' It was awful. "

By May 11, the voters eliminated all but three competitors: Alabama rocker Bo Bice, Georgia rhythm and blues singer Vonzell Solomon, and Carrie. A week later, Carrie belted out Orbison's hit "Crying," as well as "Making Love Out of Nothing at All" by Air Supply, and country star Shania Twain's "Man! I Feel Like a Woman!" Vonzell countered with hits by Donna Summer as well as soul singer Aretha Franklin and pop star Dionne Warwick, while Bo offered songs by the Rolling Stones, Elton John, and heavy metal band Badlands. The voters favored Carrie and Bo, forcing Vonzell to drop out.

In just 19 weeks, Carrie had gone from small-town college student to the brink of stardom. She had competed against some

Carrie and Bo Bice share an emotional duet during the *Idol* Season 4 finale. After so many weeks of fiercely competing against each other, the showdown came with both singing two show-stopping songs. And on May 25, 2005, a triumphant Carrie was crowned the newest American Idol.

truly talented performers, and always survived to return for another week. On their TV screens, fans saw the transformation of a nervous young woman from a tiny town in Oklahoma into somebody who was definitely at ease in front of the cameras, capable of performing at a top level in front of millions of viewers. Inside, though, the tension was clearly taking its toll on Carrie. She said,

> **"While you won't typically see me get emotional on television, I often go back to my room and let my emotions loose when I'm alone. I don't spend a lot of time thinking about how I am going to win this competition. All I concern myself with is what I'm going to do for my next performance in order to stay on the show for an additional week. I just try to do my best."**

The Final Shown Down

On May 25, the show featured the final competition between Carrie and Bo. The two competitors performed a duet, then faced off against one another. Bo sang "It's a Long Long Road" by Blue Highway, a **bluegrass** group, and then "Vehicle," a 1970s hit by hard-rocking band The Ides of March. Carrie countered by returning to her roots, belting out "Independence Day," then singing a heartfelt version of "Angels Brought Me Here," a song written by Guy Sebastian, a winner of the Australian version of *Idol*.

More than 37 million TV viewers cast votes in the final round of *American Idol*. That night, they picked Carrie Underwood as the winner.

Carrie belts out a song in her signature style in one of many appearances after her *Idol* win. As she continued her journey to stardom, Carrie recorded an album and crisscrossed the country receiving awards. But sometimes the national spotlight kept her too busy, and she was homesick for Checotah.

Busy Idol

After winning the competition, Carrie found herself thrust into the national spotlight. She toured with the other *Idol* finalists and released a single, "Inside Your Heaven," which sold 170,000 copies during its first week on the market. The song hit No. 1 on the *Billboard* charts, making Carrie the first country artist to debut in the magazine's top spot.

Carrie signed lucrative endorsement deals with Hershey's chocolate and Skechers shoes, which meant she was soon back in front of the cameras, shooting TV commercials and print advertisements for the products. Through the use of some trick photography, the Hershey's commercial showed Carrie modeling five different T-shirts advertising the company's candy bars, all in the same scene.

Carrie was also much in demand as a guest star on many TV shows, making an appearance on *The Tonight Show with Jay Leno* the night after winning the *Idol* competition, and later performing on *Saturday Night Live*. The following year, as she collected awards for *Some Hearts*, she was asked to perform on the award presentation shows, including the 2007 Grammy Awards. She recalled,

> **❝*Saturday Night Live* was really cool. It was great to be added to the list of such great iconic artists who have performed on the show before. And of course, being on stage at the Grammys—that was an amazing moment. Who'd have thought? But each one runs together. I'd love to revel in the moment a little more sometimes.❞**

Homesick for Oklahoma

Soon after winning the competition, Carrie had the opportunity to collect her *American Idol* prizes, including a new Ford Mustang and use of a private jet for a year. The big prize in the competition, though, was the recording contract—it guaranteed her $1 million in royalties from her first album. That summer and fall, she worked alongside the songwriting and production team put together by *American Idol* creator Simon Fuller to produce the album *Some Hearts*, which was released in November and immediately became a smash hit.

Although Fuller realized Carrie had great crossover potential and that her music would appeal to pop fans, Carrie wanted to make sure her first album would include mostly country songs. "I wanted the type of contract to do a country record," she said. "That's where my heart is."

One of the songs on the album is titled "Don't Forget to Remember Me." As soon as Carrie heard the song, she knew

After winning *American Idol,* Carrie made many commercials and hit the TV talk show circuit, shown here on the *Ellen Degeneres Show.* Carrie thought it was especially cool to join the list of famous artists who have shared the stage of the late-night comedy show *Saturday Night Live.*

instantly that she wanted to record it. The lyrics tell the story of a young woman who leaves home for the first time and the loneliness she feels living away from her family. To Carrie, the song said a lot about her own experience on the road and her close relationship with her mother. Said Carrie,

❝The first time I heard it, I cried because I was feeling homesick . . . . In that moment, I knew that no matter how hard it would be to get through, I had to record it. ❞

Range as a Singer

Some Hearts showed Carrie's range as a singer and her maturation as a performer. The music critics were generally positive in their reviews of the album. "Big, throbby voices and show-stopping climaxes inevitably prevail on *American Idol* and a winner this year, Carrie Underwood, brings them to country on her debut album," declared *New York Times* critic Jon Pareles. Said *Billboard* critics Ray Waddell and Jonathan Cohen, "She may have a nice platform to kick off her career, but ultimately Underwood will

Carrie's debut album *Some Hearts*, which showcased her powerful voice, was praised by many music critics and showed how Carrie's range and talent had grown. Her early success proved Simon Cowell's prediction that Carrie would go on to become an amazing country-pop star.

be a star because of her own considerable talents." And *People* magazine's music critic wrote,

> **"The fiddles at the beginning of Carrie Underwood's debut album tells you that you can take the gal out of Checotah, Oklahoma, but you can't take Checotah out of the gal. No doubt this disc shows exactly where the *American Idol* champ's heart is, as she fulfills Simon Cowell's prediction by becoming a credible country-pop artist. "**

THANKSGIVING DAY TRADITION

One of the highlights of Carrie's year as the reigning champion of *American Idol* was performing at the Macy's Thanksgiving Day parade in New York City. Known for its huge helium-filled balloons that are led down Broadway in midtown Manhattan, the parade is one of the oldest Thanksgiving traditions in America. It was launched in 1924, staged by volunteers who worked at Macy's New York department store.

Carrie, who was featured on a float with the Pillsbury Doughboy, performed the title track from her album *Some Hearts*. Coincidentally, Carrie's home state of Oklahoma sponsored its own float in the parade to mark the 100th anniversary of Oklahoma statehood. Singer and actress Kristen Chenoweth performed on the float. Among the famous Oklahomans who also rode atop the float were football coach Barry Switzer, former baseball stars Johnny Bench and Bobby Mercer, opera star Leona Mitchell, and music composer Jimmy Webb.

The album included one controversial tune—"Before He Cheats." Fans found the song as well as its video somewhat shocking given Carrie's squeaky-clean image. The song told about a girlfriend taking revenge on her cheating boyfriend, smashing his car with a baseball bat, and committing other acts of vandalism.

Critics gave high marks to the song, though, praising Carrie for the courage to step away from her image to reveal an edgier side of her personality. Said Pareles, "Ms. Underwood is such a goody-goody throughout the album that it's relief when, in 'Before He Cheats,' she defaces and smashes a cheating boyfriend's car."

Still, Carrie felt troubled by her fans' reaction to the song and included a statement on her Web site explaining that she is not the type of person who would vandalize property.

Dating a Cowboy

Soon after the album was released, Carrie hit the tour circuit again, spending six months on the road promoting *Some Hearts.* In many of the tour venues, she opened for bigger stars, including Kenny Chesney. She found it particularly thrilling to share the stage with Chesney and the other major country stars, whose work she long admired. As for Chesney, he admitted to being awed by Carrie's talent. "She connects with the audience in ways most new acts take years to develop," he said.

Meanwhile, as a major recording star, she soon found herself pursued by the **tabloid** press. Before winning the *American Idol* competition, Carrie had dated Drake Clark, her college sweetheart, but after winning the contest and going on tour, Carrie and Clark grew apart and eventually split up. She soon met Tony Romo, quarterback for the Dallas Cowboys, and suddenly the two became an item.

Her relationship with Tony lasted into 2007 before the pair decided to break up, shortly after an incident involving Carrie at Texas Stadium. On Christmas Day in 2006, the Cowboys were slated to play the Philadelphia Eagles. A few hours before the game, Tony took time away from his pre-game warm-up to meet Carrie on the field. TV cameras caught Carrie and Tony embracing and sharing a laugh. Later that day, the Eagles thrashed the Cowboys by a score of 23-7 in the nationally televised game.

After Tony had one of his worst days as a pro quarterback, fans, commentators, and sports writers wondered whether he should have been paying more attention that afternoon to the Eagles and less attention to Carrie. And then, a few weeks later, Tony cost his team a playoff win when he fumbled the ball during what should have been a game-winning field goal. Again, critics wondered whether Tony's mind was truly on the game—or on dating Carrie.

After the relationship ended, Carrie said the uproar following the game against the Eagles was definitely a factor in the breakup because Tony took the criticism about his play to heart. She said,

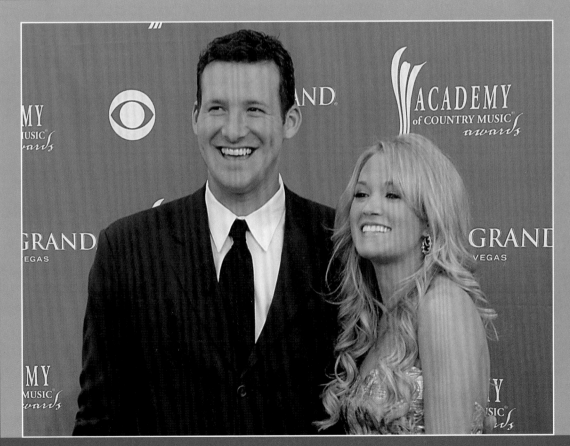

Carrie and Tony Romo of the Dallas Cowboys dated in 2006 and soon were the focus of the tabloid press. Romo was criticized during a Cowboys game for paying more attention to Carrie than to football. The media attention that resulted may have contributed to their breakup in 2007.

" Point blank, he is about football. I don't know if it's that I'm not quite his type of whatever, but I don't think he's at the point in his life where he would be willing to sacrifice football. He hated so much that people thought that he was paying more attention to me and that was causing him to not do well. **"**

Supporting Animal Rights

Away from the tabloid headlines, Carrie devoted herself to music as well as her charitable efforts. Just a few weeks after Carrie won the *Idol* competition, Hurricane Katrina swept through Louisiana and Mississippi, devastating thousands of homes. While government and charitable aid helped the thousands of people who suddenly found themselves homeless, Carrie became aware of the other victims of the hurricane—the many animals left behind by their owners to fend for themselves in the devastated communities.

Carrie helped the Humane Society of the United States raise money for relief efforts so these dogs, cats, and other animals could be captured and found new homes. Along with actors Sean Astin, Joe Mantegna, comedian Bill Maher, and other celebrities, Carrie appeared in a series of public service advertisements asking for donations to help save the animals caught in the devastation left behind by the hurricane.

By the time Carrie joined the relief effort, her devotion to the welfare of animals was well known. In fact, during an *Idol* telecast Carrie wore a T-shirt that read "V is for Vegetarian," a political statement that resulted in her election by People for the Ethical Treatment of Animals (PETA) as "World's Sexiest Vegetarian" for 2005. (She won the honor again in 2007.)

Some of her fans found it unusual that Carrie would become a vegetarian, given that she grew up on a cattle ranch, but Carrie stood by her principles. She maintained,

Carrie has always been an animal lover. After Hurricane Katrina, she helped the Humane Society raise money to find homes for animals left behind by their owners. Her deep concern for animals led to her election as 's Sexiest Vegetarian by People for the Ethical Treatment of Animals in 2005 and 2007.

COSMO *girl* PROM

INSIDE!
4-Month Prom Calendar!

WOW!
936 WAYS TO LOOK AMAZING FOR PROM!
Gorgeous Dresses, Jewelry, Hairstyles, Makeup & More!

ha! ha! ha!
Guys' Most Mortifying Prom Moments!

Get Toned

Carrie Underwood

In 2006 Carrie graced the covers of several magazines, including *Cosmo Prom Girl*. In spite of her busy schedule, she was thrilled to finish college with high honors. Although she was afraid her celebrity might affect the graduation ceremonies, Carrie proudly received her diploma with little fanfare.

"I quit eating beef when I was somewhere between 10 and 13 because we do have cows and I did bottle feed them and stuff like that. They were like my pets. . . . Later on, my

neighbor had pigs, and I thought they were cute, and it just kind of went on and on from there. I phased it out over a period of time."

Receiving Her Degree

As she toured with the other *Idol* finalists, then worked hard to produce *Some Hearts*, Carrie still found time to take the final few courses she needed to graduate from Northeastern State University. On May 6, 2006, she returned to the campus in Tahlequah to participate in the graduation exercises and receive her degree in mass communication. She graduated **magna cum laude**, a distinction bestowed on top students.

That day, she donned a **cap and gown** and joined about 1,800 Northeastern State students in the graduation procession. Actually, in the weeks preceding the commencement, the student newspaper at Northeastern State published an article questioning whether Carrie should participate in the graduation exercises, suggesting that her presence on campus would draw too much attention away from the solemn nature of the ceremony. As she accepted her diploma, Carrie expected to hear some boos in the crowd, but none materialized. "I was just another graduate," she said.

ENTERTAINING THE TROOPS

By the time Carrie won the 2005 *American Idol* competition, American troops had already been at war in Iraq for more than two years. As 2006 closed, Carrie left for Iraq to perform on a tour for American troops serving in the Middle East. The trip was sponsored by United Service Organizations, a non-profit group that has been staging shows to entertain American troops overseas since World War II.

Carrie spent a week in the Middle East, performing for American troops first at Camp Buehring in Kuwait, a small country that borders Iraq. She next visited two outposts in Iraq, Camp Speicher in the town of Tikrit and Camp Anaconda in Balad. While in Balad, she also visited wounded troops at the Air Force Field Hospital.

Carrie Underwood performs at the 41st Annual Country Music Association Awards in Nashville, Tennessee, 2007. As her fame continued to grow, Carrie kept up with a fast-paced schedule—touring, participating in charity events, and writing songs for her next album.

No Time to Slow Down

In the spring of 2007, Carrie returned to *American Idol* to make a guest appearance. Fans were shocked by what they saw—it looked as though Carrie had lost a lot of weight. Soon, rumors circulated in the tabloids and on the Internet that Carrie suffered from **anorexia nervosa**, an eating disorder.

Victims of anorexia are often teenage girls and young women who eat very little because they are concerned about gaining weight. The condition can become fatal if it is ignored—victims have been known to cause damage to their hearts and other organs as they starve themselves. Rumors about Carrie suffering from anorexia were heightened when she told a magazine in a May 2008 interview that she worries about gaining weight because it could hurt her career. "If I put on five pounds it's noticed immediately," she said.

A few months later, Carrie finally addressed the rumors and denied that she suffers from an eating disorder, explaining that she gained a lot of weight during the months of competing on *American Idol*, mostly by eating a lot of quick meals and junk food. After the show, she went back on a normal diet, exercised, and lost weight. She assured her fans that she is not anorexic, saying,

> **"I gained weight on the show, but I didn't starve myself afterward. I may think about it a little too much. I might feel guilty if I eat a pizza. But I've tried to be healthy and exercise as much as I can. If that's made me lose weight, I guess I needed to."**

CARRIE IN WAX

In 2008, Carrie's likeness in a life-size wax figure was unveiled at the world famous Madame Tussauds, the wax museum on Times Square in New York City. First established in Paris in 1761, Madame Tussauds has opened wax museums in many major world cities. Movie stars, recording stars, political figures, and other celebrities are featured in exhibits that look uncannily lifelike.

To fashion the wax figure, artists from Madame Tussauds met with Carrie several times while she toured in 2008. Carrie posed with her hands resting on her hips. At the Madame Tussauds museum, the wax figure wears the same dress that Carrie wore to the 2006 Country Music Association awards, which Carrie graciously donated to the museum.

Doing Good

In early 2007, Carrie went on tour again—this time as part of *American Idol*'s charity tour, Idol Gives Back. The tour took Carrie to South Africa; a song she recorded for the tour album, "I'll Stand

Carrie unveils her wax figure at Madame Tussauds in New York on October 22, 2008. The very lifelike figure the same sequined dress Carrie had worn to the 2006 Country Music Association awards, which Carrie had donated to the museum.

By You," was released as a single exclusively as an MP3 download, and soon hit No. 2 on iTunes. In 2008, she took part in the Idol Gives Back tour again and also participated in other charity events, including performing in the 2008 Stand Up To Cancer campaign.

She has also recorded a new version of Mötley Crüe's hit "Home Sweet Home" for use as the *American Idol* theme for contestants who are voted off the show. The song was made available for downloads by MP3 distributors, and Carrie agreed to donate a percentage of her royalties from the song to the Humane Society. Said Carrie,

> ❝I've always loved this song, and besides being very fitting for *Idol*, to me, the title is also very fitting with animal rescue and finding animals their own homes. So we felt it was important to tie the release into an amazing animal charity like the Humane Society of the United States.❞

Not Ready to Settle Down

Meanwhile, after her split up with Tony Romo she dated TV actor Chace Crawford, but by early 2008 the tabloids reported that Carrie was in a relationship with Travis Stork, a physician, TV host, and one-time star of *The Bachelor*. By early 2009, Carrie had been linked romantically to Mike Fisher, a star player for the Ottawa Senators of the National Hockey League. In fact, Carrie could

Carrie put her all into recording her second album, *Carnival Ride*. It went double platinum, and three singles rocketed to the top of the country charts. Critics praised Carrie for offering more edgy, feisty songs and for keeping her musical momentum going strong.

occasionally be seen at the arenas where the Senators competed, caught on the JumboTrons as she watched the games. Said Mike's close friend and fitness coach Tony Greco, "I think it's serious. I mean, he's really happy with her. They're a perfect match."

For her part, Carrie insisted on keeping her private life out of the tabloids, although she acknowledged that she isn't ready yet to make a commitment to any relationship. Carrie said she still has a lot she wants to accomplish musically before taking a break to raise a family—she has no intentions of trying to raise young children on a tour bus. At this point, though, those days are still a bit in the future.

> **"That's definitely the plan, but you never know what God has in store for you. Now, keep in mind, that I'm nowhere near getting married or having children. That's a long way away."**

Praise for *Carnival Ride*

Carrie certainly made it clear in 2007 that she has a lot more to accomplish musically when she released her second album, *Carnival Ride*. Three singles from the album hit the top of the country charts, and by the end of the year the album was certified double platinum.

Unlike *Some Hearts*, Carrie took a more active role in writing songs for the album, helping to write the music and lyrics for 4 of the 13 tracks on the CD. Critics praised the effort, giving Carrie high marks for taking on edgier songs in *Carnival Ride*, showing a more troubled soul than the songs on *Some Hearts* would suggest.

"Carrie Underwood showed how good she is when she gets feisty on 'Before He Cheats,' the biggest hit—and best song—off her smash debut, 2005's *Some Hearts*," wrote *People* music critic Chuck Arnold. "The finest moments on this follow-up find the *American Idol* champ raising some more hell." Writing in *Rolling Stone*, critic Rob Sheffield said, "The most fun is 'Last Name' where she . . . runs off to Vegas with a guy she doesn't know. *'My mama would be so ashamed'*—now that sounds like the real Carrie." And writing in *Billboard*, music critic Ken Tucker said,

> **"After [her] debut album . . . Carrie Underwood is under significant pressure to keep the momentum going. Luckily, the Oklahoman delivers in spades on her sophomore effort, on which she was much more involved in the creative process. First single 'So Small,' No. 4 on *Billboard*'s Hot Country Songs chart, is a soaring song about the important things in life. 'Just a Dream' is the tale of the death of a young soldier from the perspective of his girl back home. . . . Underwood provides a growling and gritty vocal on the defiant 'Flat on the Floor' and convincingly covers Randy Travis' 1988 hit 'I Told You So,' which has long deserved a second life. If only every follow-up was this good."**

CARRIE AT THE OPRY

The theater in Nashville known as the Grand Ole Opry House is regarded as one of the most important places in country music. Starting as a weekly country music radio show in 1925, the *Grand Ole Opry* became so popular that sponsors erected a 500-seat concert hall seven years later to stage the acts broadcast over the air. That auditorium proved to be too small, and the *Opry* moved around for decades. In 1974, the current home, the Grand Ole Opry House, was opened providing seating for more than 4,000 people. Broadcasts of the *Opry* are syndicated on 200 radio stations each week.

To perform on the Grand Old Opry House stage, performers have to be invited by other members and then inducted into the Opry. To be inducted into the Opry is considered an honor for a country singer. In 2008, Carrie was invited into the Opry cast by country singer Randy Travis. She was inducted on May 10 by singer Garth Brooks, who presented her with the induction award—a 14-inch bronze replica of an Opry microphone stand. "This really seems like a great family to be a part of," Carrie said that night. "I promise I'll do everything I possibly can to not make you regret it."

Carrie enjoys a 2008 pre-Grammy party with singer Leona Lewis and music executive Clive Davis. At the Grammys, Carrie's blockbuster single, "Last Name," was awarded Best Female Country Vocal Performance. She won over other talented country singers, including her idol Martina McBride.

For her work on the album, Carrie would go on to win Female Vocalist of the Year at the 2008 Country Music Association awards. In addition to winning the award, she hosted the nationally televised program. She also won honors for the album at the 2009 People's Choice Awards and at the Grammy Awards. At the Grammys, Carrie won the award for Best Female Country Vocal Performance for the single "Last Name." The other nominees included her idol, Martina McBride, as well as other top country singers, including LeAnn Rimes, Lee Ann Womack, and Trisha Yearwood. Carrie also performed the song during the telecast. When she accepted the award, Carrie said, "There's no way this could possibly on this planet get old!"

Entertainer of the Year

On Sunday, April 5, 2009, the 44th Annual Academy of Country Music Awards ceremony took place in Las Vegas, Nevada, and it was there that Carrie beat out country music's best to take the top honor. In a fan-voted category, she became the first woman since 2001 to be named ACM Entertainer of the Year. Upon receiving the award, a teary-eyed Carrie said:

> **I've had a lot of good moments in the last four years. This one takes the cake!**

Earlier in the evening, Carrie also won the award for top female vocalist, and upon accepting that trophy she said,

> **I feel like I just won *American Idol* all over again. . . . Thank you Simon Fuller.**

New Challenges Ahead

Carrie has made plans to release a third album. Clearly, she wants to take even more of a hand in writing songs for her next album than she did on her previous two albums. She said,

> **I'm getting more comfortable with my writing abilities. I know that they're there now. In the beginning, I was like, 'I'll try it, and if I can't I won't mess with it again.' But I'm not one of those people that has to write every song because there are so many people out there who are great writers. But it is important to at least try.**

Carrie also realizes that since *Some Hearts* and *Carnival Ride* were so popular among her fans, she will be under tremendous pressure to produce a third album that would live up to the achievements, both critically and in terms of sales, as her first two efforts. "I have two good albums under my belt, and now I can focus on what I really want to do and say," she said.

Despite her meteoric rise to stardom, which has occurred over the course of just a handful of years, Carrie still believes she is the

Carrie proudly shows off her 2009 Academy of Country Music (ACM) Awards. She was overjoyed to be named both ACM Entertainer of the Year and Best Female Vocalist. Only four years after she won *American Idol,* Carrie has truly become a superstar.

March 30, 2009

CASHBOX

magazine, inc.

®™

Carrie Underwood

Top Country Singles
#1. I Told You So (f. Randy Travis)
Top Country Albums
#1. Carnival Ride
Top Popular Singles
#7. I Told You So (f. Randy Travis)

THE TOP
MUSIC CHARTS
MUSIC NEWS
CD REVIEWS
INDIE ARTISTS
CELEBRITY INTERVIEWS
STREAMING RADIO
MORE AND...

Carrie's journey to stardom has been fast, but she feels she is still a small-town girl from Oklahoma and is firmly grounded by family and friends. At the same time, Carrie is focusing on her bright future. Judging from her past efforts, the young singer will continue to delight fans for many years to come.

THE AMERICAN IDOL EXPERIENCE

Visitors to Disney World in Orlando, Florida, can find out what it's like to compete on *American Idol* by participating in the American Idol Experience, an attraction at the theme park that enables participants to audition in front of a panel of judges as well as a live audience. Just like the TV show, the audience members vote for the top performer of the day, with the winner rewarded with an opportunity to audition in front of *American Idol* producers.

Carrie and 2008 *American Idol* winner David Cook performed a duet in 2009 to help launch the attraction. Said Disney Parks chairman Jay Rasulo, "Our goal is to try to recreate the excitement of those 24 people who show up on that *American Idol* stage. We believe many, many viewers want to know exactly how it feels, and we're going to try to reproduce that feeling for them."

same small-town girl from Checotah she was on that day in 2005 when she made the eight-hour drive to St. Louis to audition for *American Idol*. Carrie now lives in Nashville, shares the stage with the top names in country music, and has attained enormous wealth and fame, but she also enjoys a home life and getting together with family members and friends. She says,

"I have two lives. There's 'Carrie Underwood' the singer who walks the red carpets. Then there's 'Carrie' the girl in sweats sitting home watching TV with her dog. I'm 'Carrie' 90 percent of the time. I was at a family reunion over Christmas, and my little cousins, whom I hadn't seen in a couple of years, kept calling me 'Carrie Underwood . . . Carrie Underwood, come over here!' I was like, 'Sweetie, I'm your cousin. My name is Carrie.' I have to remind everybody that 'Carrie Underwood' exists on the red carpet and onstage, but 'Carrie' exists everywhere else."

1983 Carrie Underwood born in Muskogee, Oklahoma, on March 10.

1986 Sings in public for the first time during a church recital.

1996 Becomes a vegetarian.

1997 Auditions for a recording contract at Capitol Records.

2001 Graduates from Checotah High School.

Enrolls in Northeastern State University.

2002 *American Idol* premiers on the Fox network.

Carrie attends college and works as a gas station cashier.

2005 Competes on *American Idol* and, on May 25, is voted winner at the conclusion of the show's fourth season.

Releases first album, *Some Hearts*.

2006 Graduates with a degree in mass communication from Northeastern State University.

Performs concerts for troops serving in Iraq and Kuwait.

2007 Releases second album, *Carnival Ride*, on October 23.

2008 Inducted into the Grand Old Opry.

2009 Helps launch American Idol Experience at Disney World in Orlando, Florida.

2005   Voted winner of *American Idol.*

2006   *Some Hearts* wins Billboard Album of the Year and Country Album of the Year; Carrie wins Female Billboard 200 Artist of the Year, Female Country Artist of the Year, and New Country Artist of the Year.

"Jesus Take the Wheel" named Recorded Song of the Year by the Gospel Music Association.

"Jesus Take the Wheel" named Country Music Television's Breakthrough Video of the Year and Female Video of the Year.

Selected Female Vocalist of the Year by the Country Music Association and also selected for the association's Horizon Award for best new artist.

Academy of Country Music names "Jesus Take the Wheel" Single of the Year and Carrie as Top New Female Vocalist and Top Female Vocalist while *Some Hearts* wins Album of the Year.

2007   Awarded Grammys for Best Female Country Vocal Performance and Best Country Song for "Jesus Take the Wheel."

"Before He Cheats" wins Video of the Year and Female Video of the Year by Country Music Television.

"Before He Cheats" selected Single of the Year by the Country Music Association while Carrie wins Female Vocalist of the Year.

2008   "Before He Cheats" wins Grammy as Country Song of the Year.

Selected Top Female Vocalist by Academy of Country Music.

Selected Female Vocalist of the Year by Country Music Association.

2009   Wins People's Choice Awards for Favorite Female Singer and Favorite Country Song for "Last Name."

Wins Grammy Award for Best Female Country Vocal Performance for "Last Name."

Selected Female Vocalist of the Year by Country Music Association and voted Entertainer of the Year by country music fans.

anorexia nervosa—Mental illness that prompts patients to lose their appetites, often motivated by fears of gaining weight. Anorexia nervosa mostly afflicts teenage girls and young women.

bluegrass—Style of country music featuring heavy reliance on stringed instruments, including guitars, banjos, and fiddles.

cap and gown—Traditional dress worn at graduation exercises, usually featuring a long robe with wide sleeves and a square, flat-topped cap known as a mortarboard.

disco—Style of dance music popularized during the 1970s that features pulsating rhythms played on electronically amplified instruments, such as electric guitars and organs.

gospel music—Music inspired by Christian themes, often celebrating the adoration of Jesus Christ.

heavy metal—Music produced on electronically amplified instruments that features loud beats, loud singing, and distorted sounds, usually performed by artists who regard themselves as outlaws of rock 'n' roll.

hospice—Medical facility that houses terminally ill patients.

magna cum laude—Latin term that means "with great praise," a distinction awarded to a university's top students.

page—Messenger, typically a high school or college student, employed by the U.S. Congress or a state legislative body.

platinum—In the music industry, a distinction awarded to an album that has sold at least a million copies.

rockabilly—Style of music combining rock 'n' roll and country sounds pioneered by such artists as Carl Perkins and Elvis Presley.

salutatorian—Student who attains the second-highest ranking in a graduating class.

tabloid—Style of journalism practiced in newspapers, TV, and the Internet that focuses on celebrity news and gossip and bizarre crimes; popularized during the 1920s by newspapers published in tabloid format, meaning they were half the size of broadsheet newspapers.

tuition—The cost of attending college or private school.

vegetarian—Person who has elected, on moral principles, not to eat meat.

Books

Kallen, Stuart A. *The History of Country Music*. Farmington Hills, Michigan: Lucent, 2002.

La Bella, Laura. *Carrie Underwood*. New York: Rosen Central, 2008.

Rich, Jason. *American Idol Season 4: Official Behind-the-Scenes Fan Book*. New York: Prima Games, 2005.

Periodicals

Bryson, Jodi. "As Fate Would Have It." *Girls' Life* vol. 12, no. 6 (June-July 2006): p. 40.

Fahner, Molly. "All-American Girl." *Cosmopolitan* vol. 245, no. 1 (July 2008): p. 26.

Price, Deborah Evans. "I'm Still the Same Person." *Country Weekly* vol. 16, no. 6 (March 23, 2009): p. 32.

Price, Deborah Evans, and Ray Waddell. "Carrie Enjoys the Ride." *Billboard* vol. 119, no. 36 (September 8, 2007): p. 26.

Schneller, Johanna. "American Girl." *InStyle* vol. 15, no. 5 (May 2008): p. 127.

Web Sites

www.americanidol.com

By accessing *American Idol*'s official Web site, fans can read biographies of the competitors, view photos and videos and read the latest news about the show and the performers. By accessing the site's Alumni News link, fans can find updates for many of the performers in *American Idol*'s past seasons.

www.carrieunderwoodofficial.com

Carrie's official Web site. Fans can read news about Carrie, access photos and videos, check on her tour schedule, and add comments to a blog.

www.nsuok.edu

Northeastern State University, the school where Carrie earned her degree in mass communications, is located in Tahlequah, Oklahoma. Visitors to the school's Web site can learn about programs of study, student life, athletics, and other facets of campus life.

www.opry.com

Official Web site for the Grand Ole Opry, the Nashville, Tennessee, theater and radio show that have evolved into institutions of American country music. Visitors can read a history of the Opry, biographies of inductees, participate in blogs, and read news and feature stories about Opry performers.

ABOUT THE AUTHOR

Hal Marcovitz is a former newspaper reporter who has written more than 100 books for young readers. In 2005, *Nancy Pelosi*, his biography of House Speaker Nancy Pelosi, was named to *Booklist* magazine's list of recommended feminist books for young readers. He lives in Chalfont, Pennsylvania, with his wife Gail and daughter Ashley.